P9-DTK-065

Draw 50 Dinosaurs
and other Prehistoric Animals

BOOKS IN THIS SERIES

Draw 50 Dinosaurs

and other Prehistoric Animals

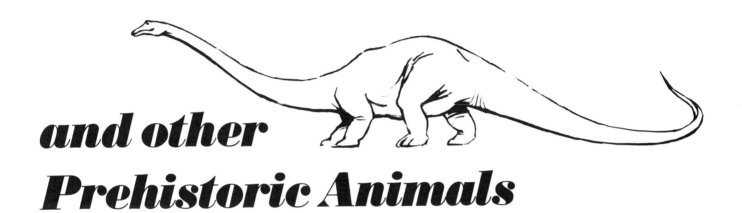

LEE J. AMES

With a Foreword by
GEORG ZAPPLER, Director, Staten Island Zoological Society

BROADWAY BOOKS
NEW YORK

BROADWAY

Published by Broadway Books
a division of Random House, Inc.

BROADWAY BOOKS and it's logo, a letter B bisected on the diagonal, are
trademarks of Broadway Books, a division of Random House, Inc.

The Library of Congress has cataloged the first printing
of this title as follows:
Ames, Lee J.
    Draw 50 dinosaurs and other prehistoric animals/Lee J.
    Ames: with a foreword by Georg Zappler.—1st ed.—Garden
City, N.Y.: Doubleday, c1977.
    [63] p.: ill.; 32 cm.
    SUMMARY: Step-by-step instructions for drawing fifty different dinosaurs
    and other prehistoric animals.

    1. Dinosauria in art.   2. Extinct animals in art.   3. Animal paintings and illus-
    tration   [1. Animal paintings and illustrations.   2. Drawing—Technique]
    I. Title.
NC780.A482   743′.6   MARC
Library of Congress   77[7712]   AC
Library of Congress Catalog Card Number 76-7285
ISBN 0-385-11134-7.
ISBN 0-385-19520-6 (PBK)

39 38 37 36 35 34 33 32

Foreword

Mr. Ames has designed a fascinating and instructive book. Young readers and adult students will be able to gain an appreciation of many of nature's now extinct life forms. But, more importantly, they will be able to re-create for themselves the kinds of animals that swam the seas, walked the land and soared through the air in ages long past. Some of these creatures were the ancestors of now living forms, others were only temporarily successful and disappeared without issue. Ponderous woolly mammoths, plated and horned dinosaurs, spiny sharks, flightless birds, membrane-winged reptiles, seagoing lizards, gigantic camels, saber-toothed cats and giant swimming scorpions all come to life again by way of step-by-step, easy-to-follow instructions. And, although the drawing sequences are very basic and simple, the final results yield scientifically accurate fleshed-out representations of animals known only from their fossil remains. In order to arrive at his reconstructions, the artist has drawn on over a hundred years of scientific research by paleontologists from all over the world. Mr. Ames is to be commended for making the world of prehistoric life accessible to everyone.

GEORG ZAPPLER
Director, Staten Island Zoological Society
(formerly with the Department of Vertebrate Paleontology
The American Museum of Natural History

To the Reader

This book will show you a way to draw prehistoric animals. You need not start with the first illustration. Choose whichever you wish. When you have decided, follow the step-by-step method shown. *Very lightly* and *carefully,* sketch out the step number one. However, this step, which is the easiest, should be done *most carefully.* Step number two is added right to step number one, also lightly and also very carefully. Step number three is sketched right on top of numbers one and two. Continue this way to the last step.

It may seem strange to ask you to be extra careful when you are drawing what seem to be the easiest first steps, but this is most important, for a careless mistake at the beginning may spoil the whole picture at the end. As you sketch out each step, watch the spaces between the lines, as well as the lines, and see that they are the same. After each step, you may want to lighten your work by pressing it with a kneaded eraser (available at art supply stores).

When you have finished, you may want to redo the final step in India ink with a fine brush or pen. When the ink is dry, use the kneaded eraser to clean off the pencil lines. The eraser will not affect the India ink.

Here are some suggestions: In the first few steps, even when all seems quite correct, you might do well to hold your work up to a mirror. Sometimes the mirror shows that you've twisted the drawing off to one side without being aware of it. At first you may find it difficult to draw the egg shapes, or ball shapes, or sausage shapes, or just to make the pencil go where you wish. Don't be discouraged. The more you practice, the more you will develop control. Use a compass if you wish; professional artists do! The only equipment you'll need will be a medium or soft pencil, paper, the kneaded eraser and, if you wish, a compass, pen or brush.

The first steps in this book are shown darker than necessary so that they can be clearly seen. (Keep your work very light.)

Remember there are many other ways and methods to make drawings. This book shows just one method. Why don't you seek out other ways from teachers, from libraries and, most importantly . . . from inside yourself?

Lee J. Ames

To the Parent or Teacher

"David can draw a dinosaur better than anybody else!" Such peer acclaim and encouragement generate incentive. Contemporary methods of art instruction (freedom of expression, experimentation, self-evaluation of competence and growth) provide a vigorous, fresh-air approach for which we must all be grateful.

New ideas need not, however, totally exclude the old. One such is the "follow me, step-by-step" approach. In my young learning days this method was so common, and frequently so exclusive, that the student became nothing more than a pantographic extension of the teacher. In those days it was excessively overworked.

This does not mean that the young hand is never to be guided. Rather, specific guiding is fundamental. Step-by-step guiding that produces satisfactory results is valuable even when the means of accomplishment are not fully understood by the student.

The novice with a musical instrument is frequently taught to play simple melodies as quickly as possible, well before he learns the most elemental scratchings at the surface of music theory. The resultant self-satisfaction, pride in accomplishment, can be a significant means of providing motivation. And all from mimicking an instructor's "Do-as-I-do. . . ."

Mimicry is prerequisite for developing creativity. We learn the use of our tools by mimicry. Then we can use those tools for creativity. To this end I would offer the budding artist the opportunity to memorize or mimic (rotelike, if you wish) the making of "pictures." "Pictures" he has been eager to be able to draw.

The use of this book should be available to anyone who *wants* to try another way of flapping his wings. Perhaps he will then get off the ground when his friend says, "David can draw a dinosaur better than anybody else!"

Lee J. Ames

Draw 50 Dinosaurs
and other Prehistoric Animals

TYRANNOSAURUS   50 feet long
A Giant Meat-eating Dinosaur

APATOSAURUS (formerly BRONTOSAURUS)   65 feet long
A Plant-eating Dinosaur

STEGOSAURUS 20 feet long
A Plated Dinosaur

PROTOCERATOPS   6 feet long
An Early Horned Dinosaur

TRICERATOPS   30 feet long
A Plant-eating Horned Dinosaur

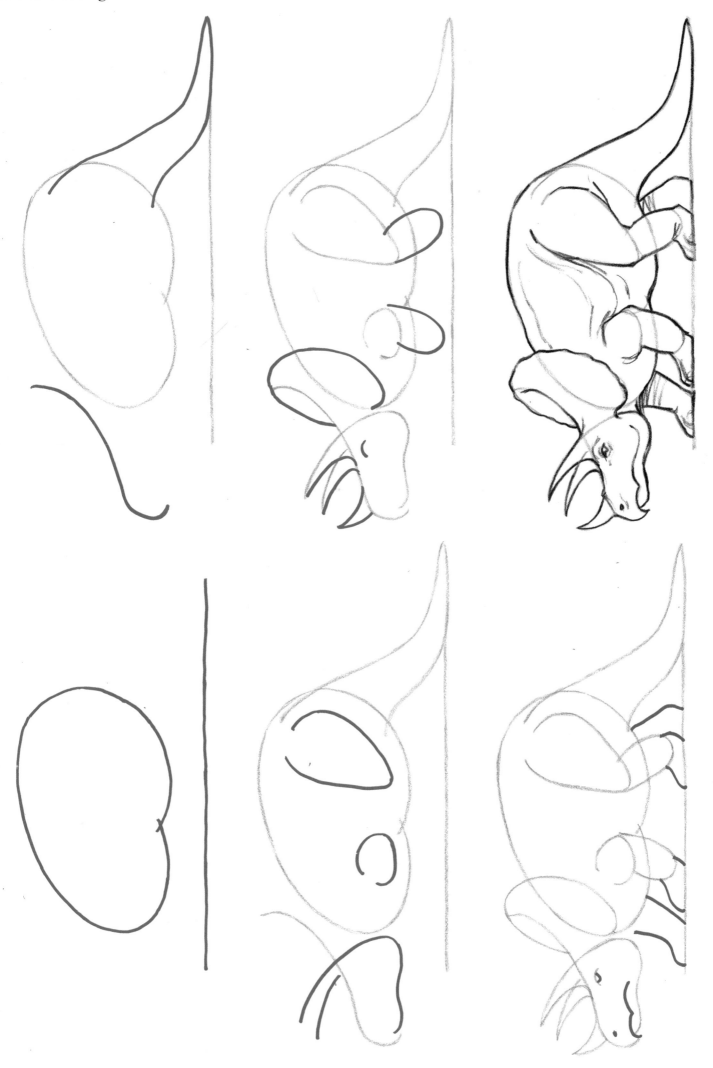

STYRACOSAURUS   16 feet long
A Plant-eating Horned Dinosaur

GUANODON   30 feet long
A Plant-eating Dinosaur

ANKYLOSAURUS ' 20 feet long
A Plant-eating Armored Dinosaur

DIPLODOCUS 87 feet long
A Giant Plant-eating Dinosaur

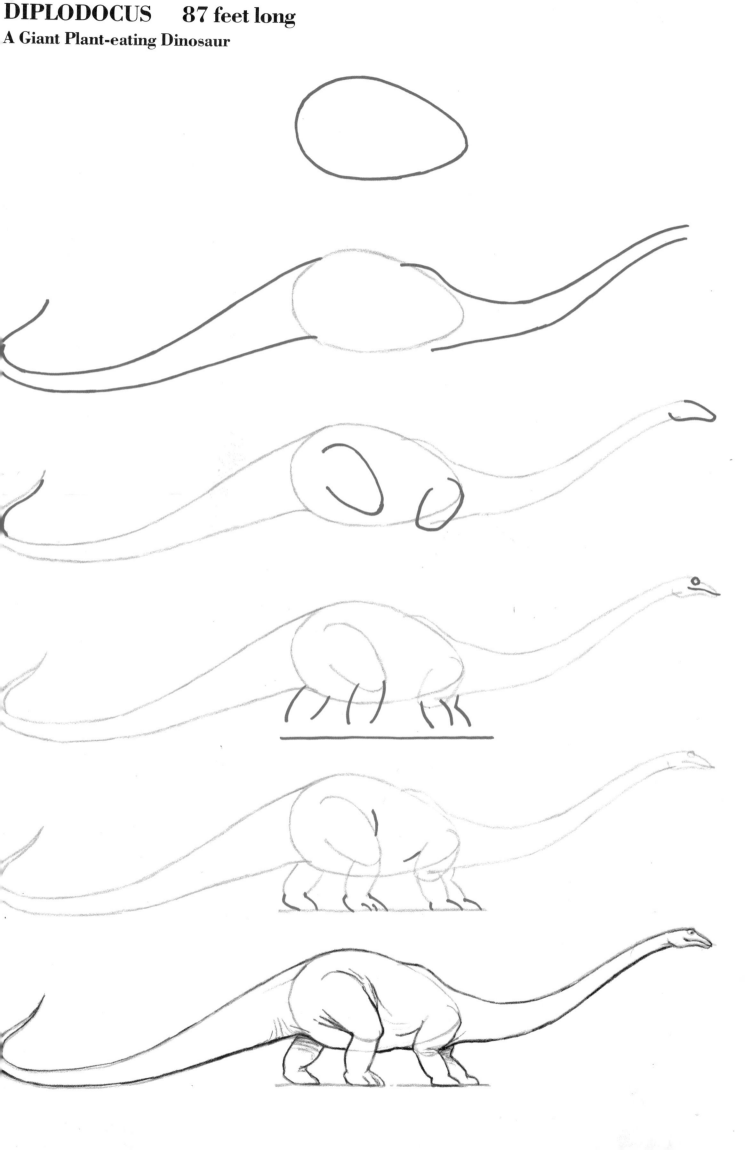

STRUTHIOMIMUS   6 feet tall
The "Ostrich" Dinosaur

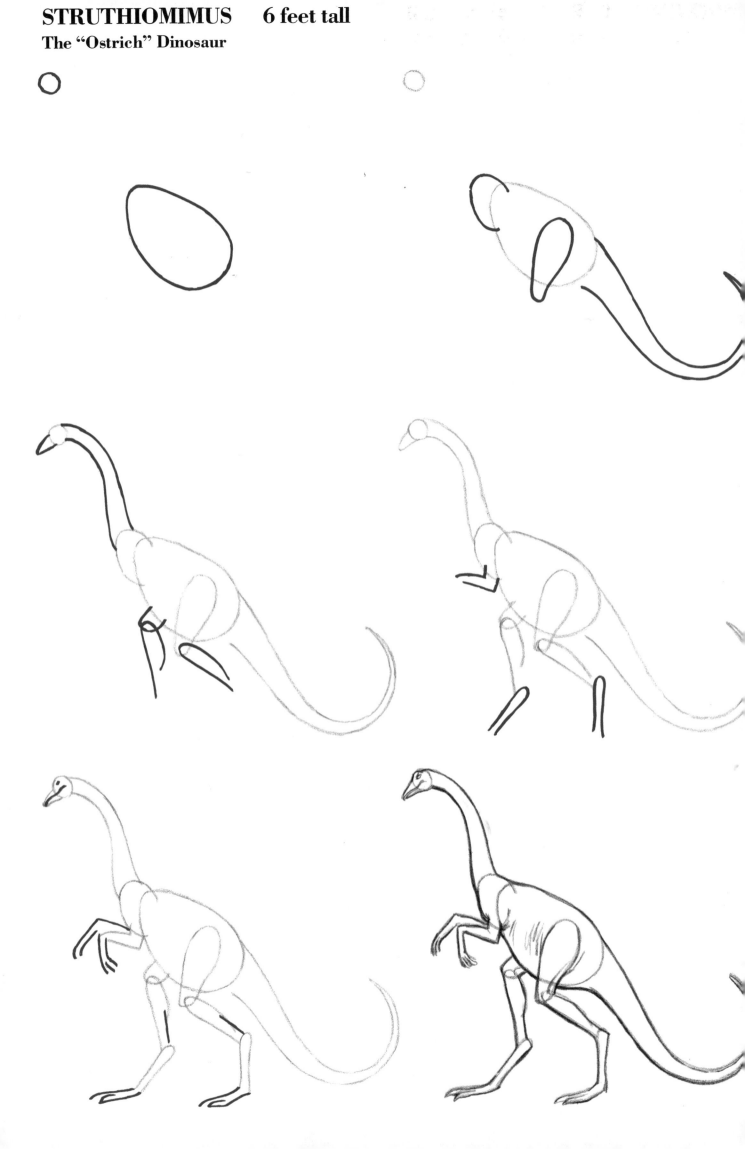

BRACHIOSAURUS   40 feet tall
The Bulkiest of the Giant Plant-eating Dinosaurs

ANATOSAURUS   30 feet long
A Duck-billed Dinosaur

A NAUTILOID   9 feet long
An Ancient Relative of Squids and Octopuses

AN AMMONOID   5 inches long
An Ancient Mollusk

A TRILOBITE   4 inches long
An Ancient Relative of the Crabs, Spiders and Insects

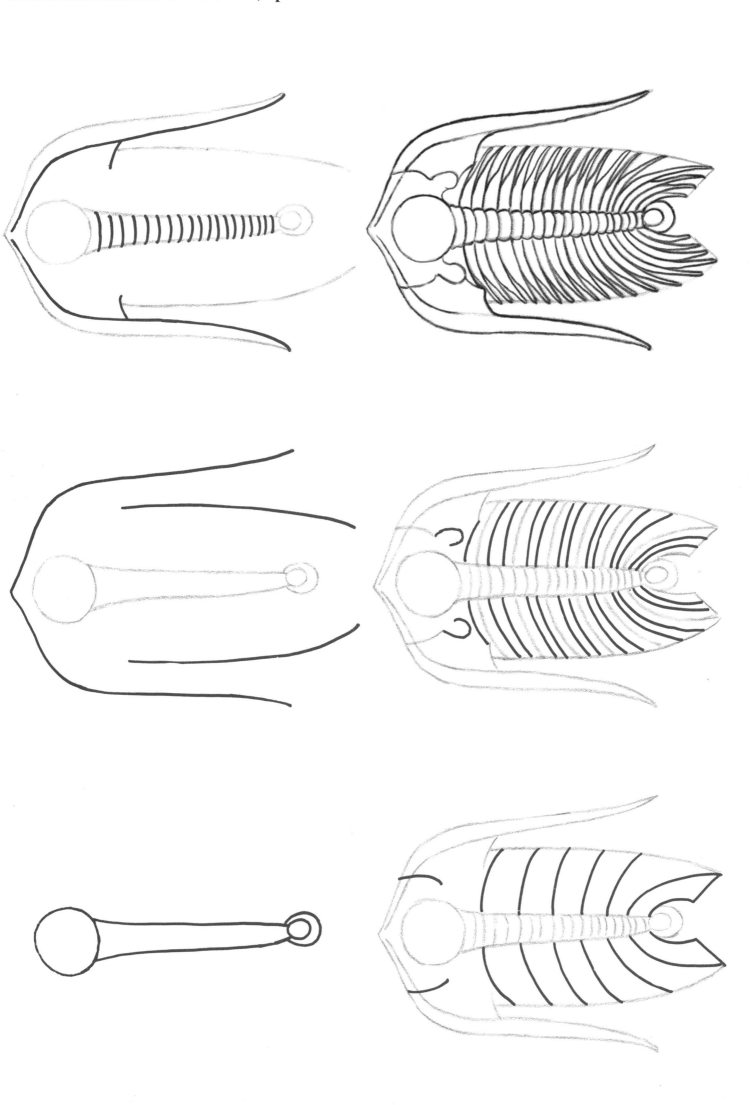

A EURYPTERID   9 feet long
A Seagoing Relative of Scorpions and Spiders

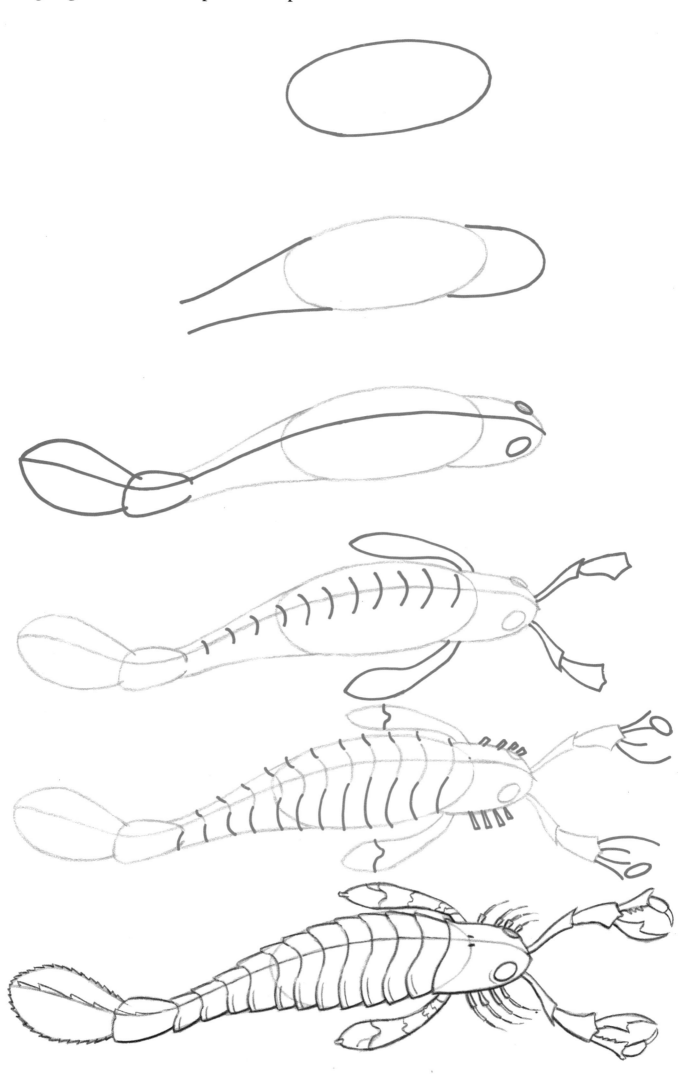

HOLOPTYCHIUS 30 inches long

An Ancient Fish, Ancestor of the Amphibians

PLEURACANTHUS   7 feet long
A Spiny Fish—Not Related to the Sharks

DINICHTHYS   30 feet long
An Ancient Giant Fish

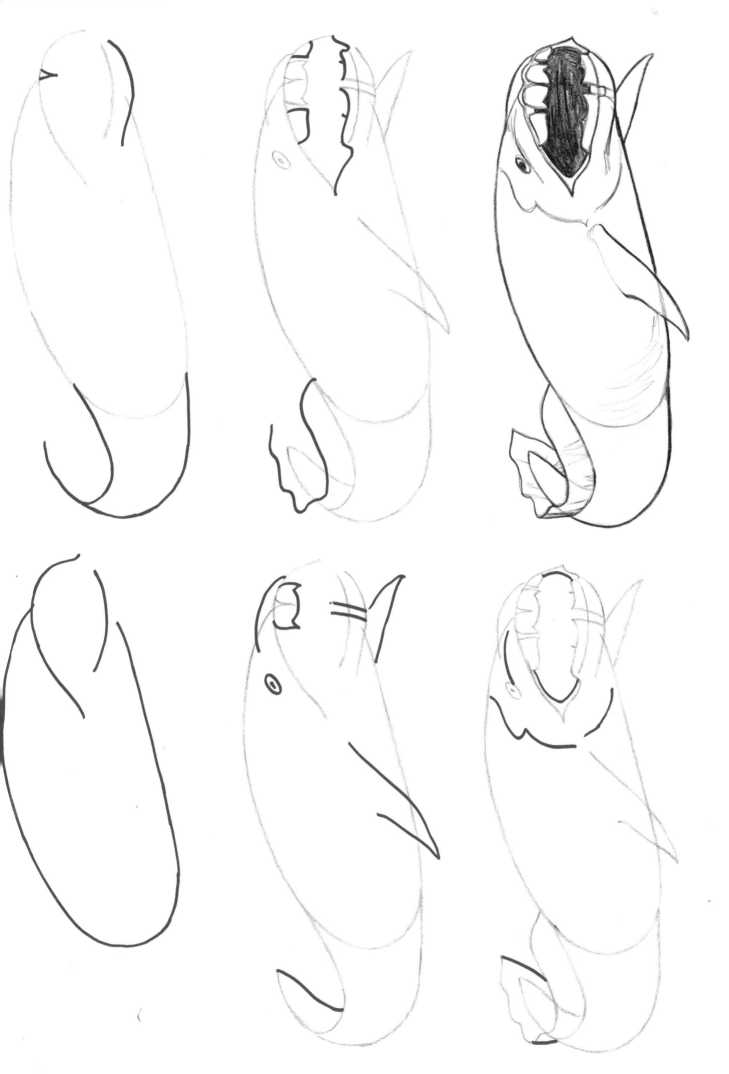

DIPLOCAULUS   2 feet long
An Early Water-living Amphibian

ERYOPS   5 feet long
An Early Land-going Amphibian, Distantly Related to Modern Frogs

MESOSAURUS   16 inches long
Early Fish-eating Reptile

CYNOGNATHUS   6 feet long
A Mammal-like Reptile

GEOSAURUS   15 feet long
A Seagoing Crocodilian

TRIMACROMERUM   10 feet long
A Short-necked Seagoing Reptile

KANNEMEYERIA   6 feet long
A Mammal-like Reptile

ELASMOSAUR   50 feet long
A Snake-necked Sea Reptile

PTERANODON   26 foot wingspread

A Tailless Membrane-winged Reptile

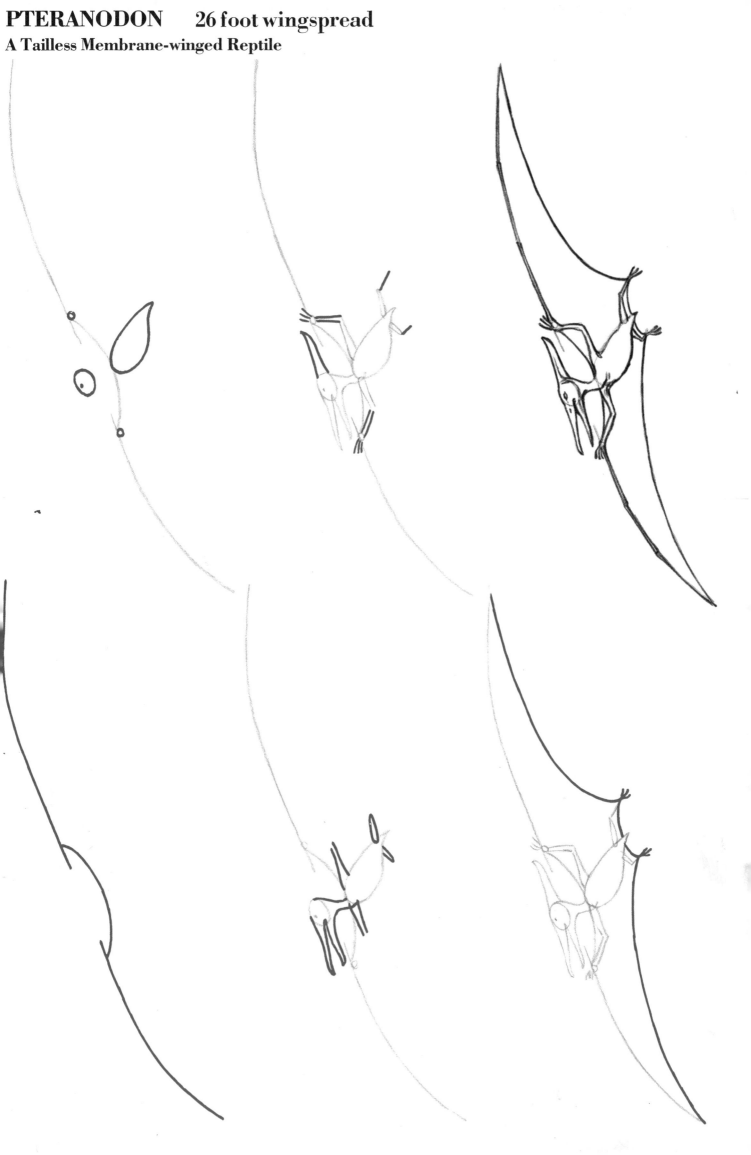

MOSASAUR   30 feet long
A Seagoing Lizard

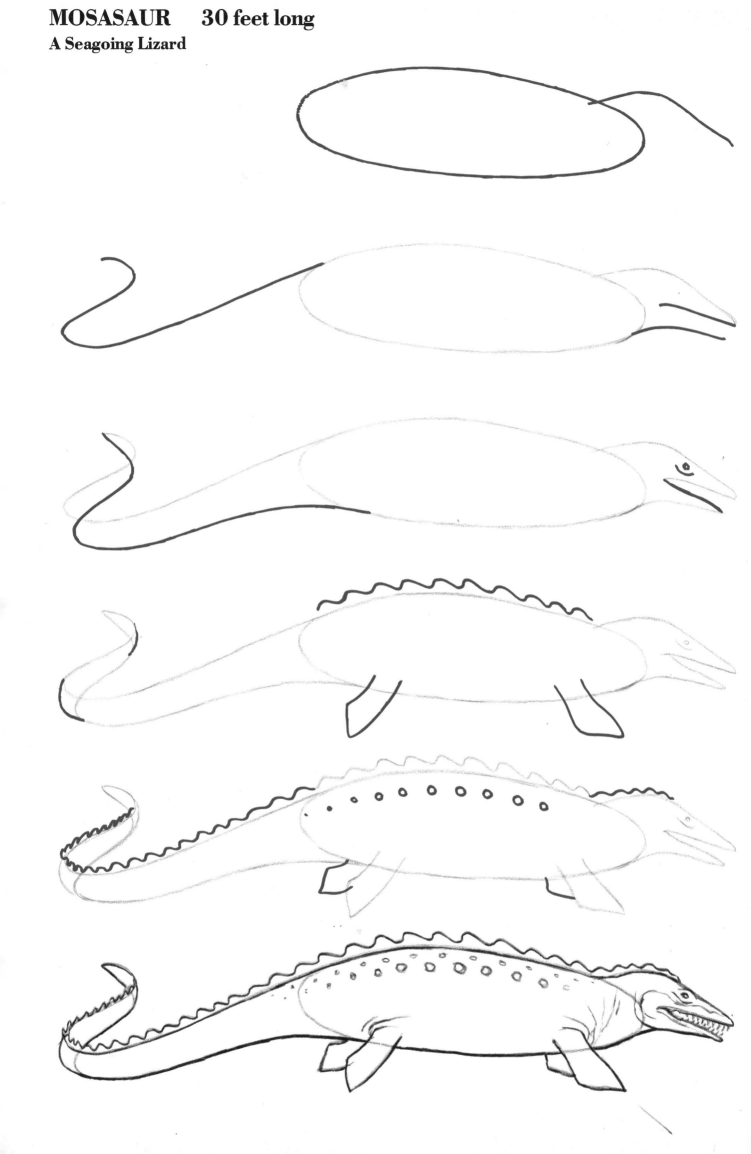

DIMETRODON   10 feet long
An Early Mammal-like Reptile

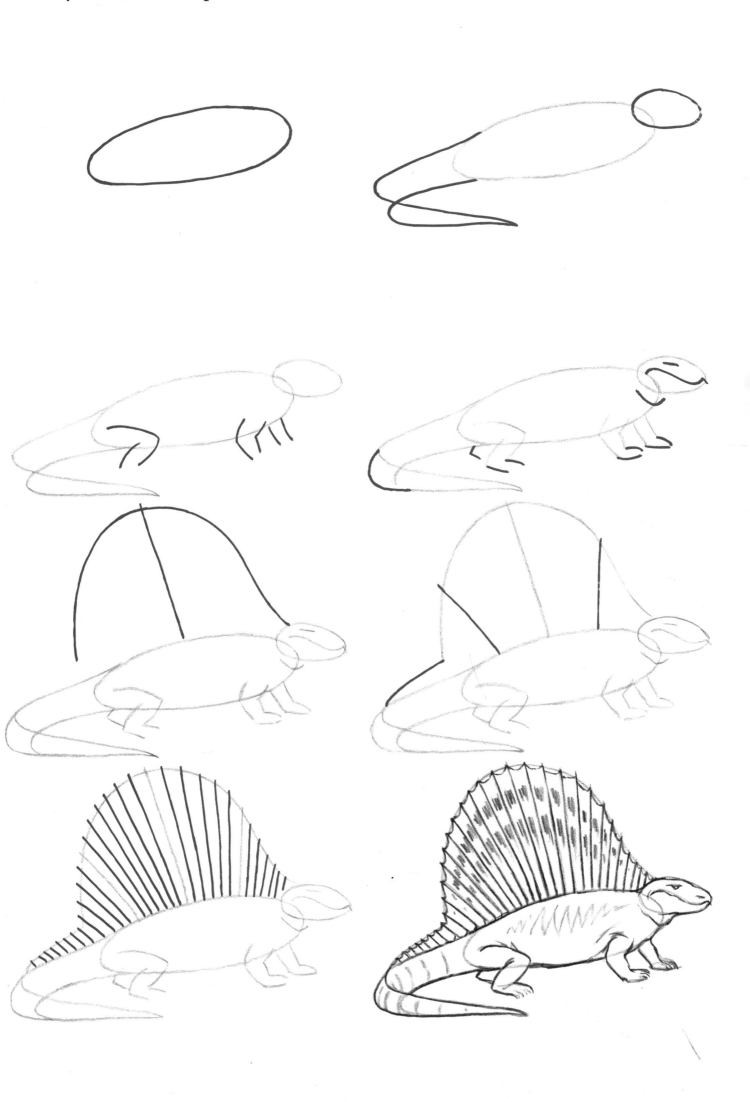

ARCHELON   12 feet long
An Ancient Sea Turtle

RHAMPHORHYNCHUS   4 feet long
A Membrane-winged Reptile

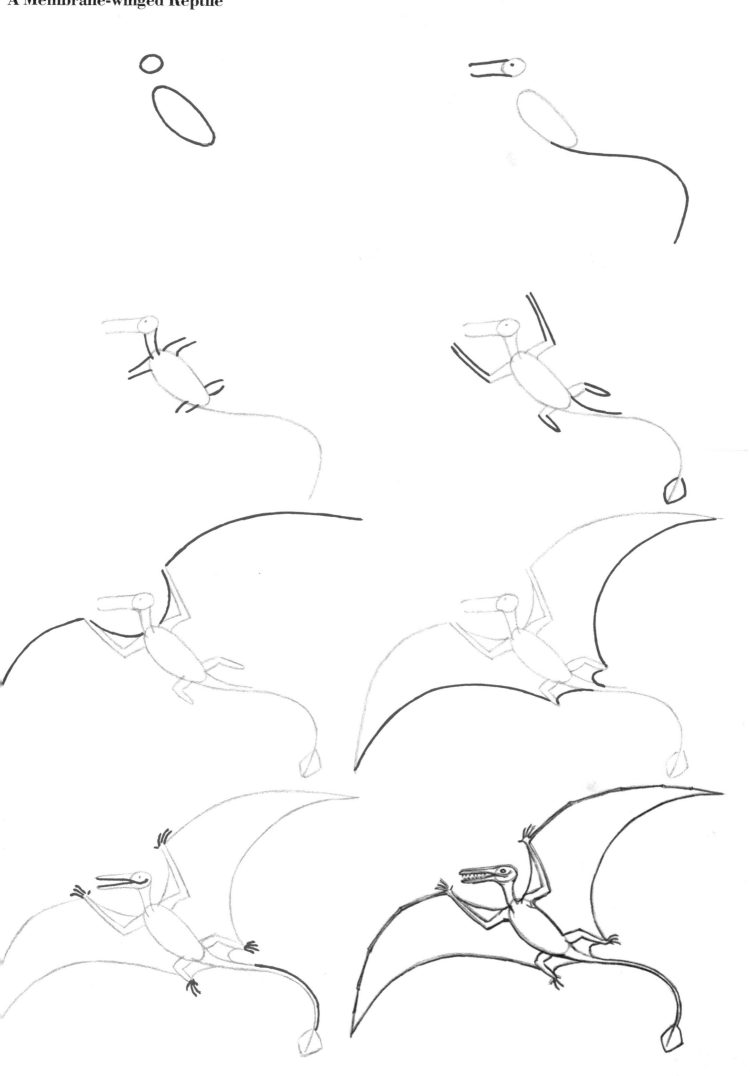

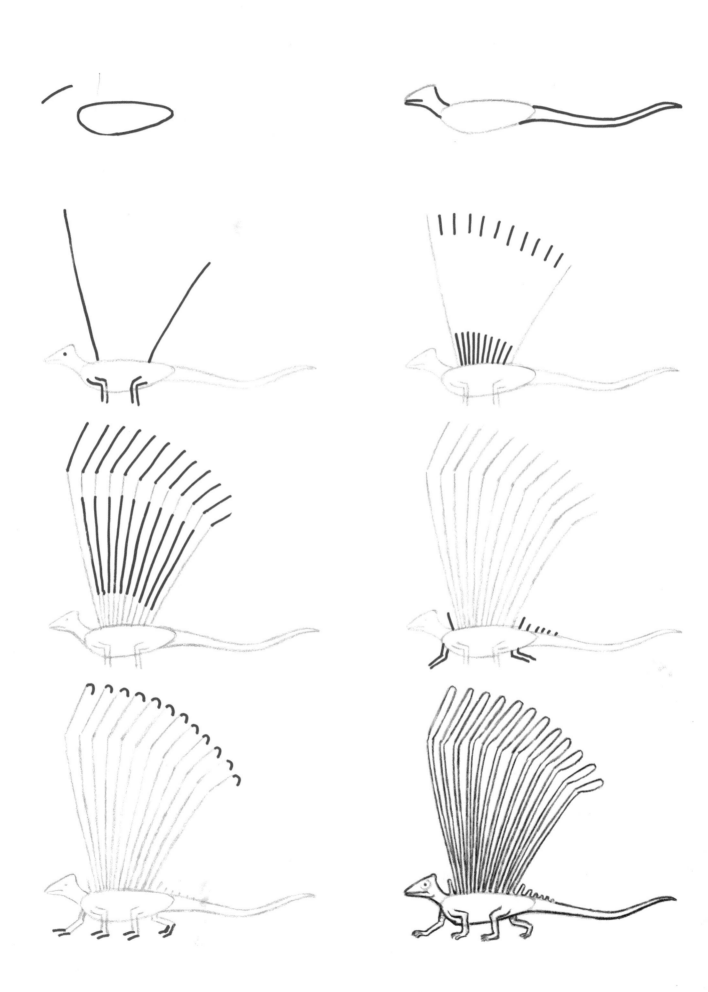

SALTOPOSUCHUS   45 inches long
A Two-legged Reptile, Ancestor of Dinosaurs and Birds

MOA   10 feet tall
A Giant Flightless Bird of New Zealand

HESPERORNIS   5 feet tall
A Primitive Toothed Diving Bird

ARCHAEOPTERYX   15 inches long
The First Bird

DIATRYMA   7 feet tall
A Meat-eating Giant Flightless Bird

SMILODON   8 feet long
A Saber-toothed Cat

GLYPTODON   9 feet long
An Ancient Relative of the Armadillo

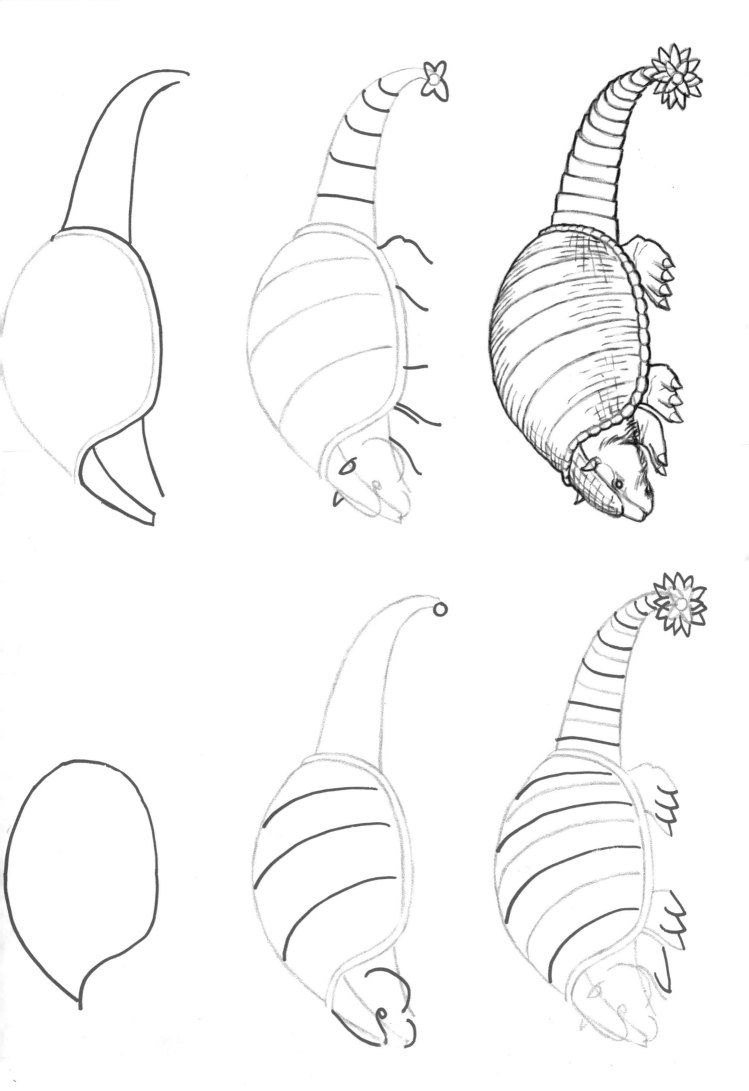

MEGALOCEROS   11 feet across the antlers
The Giant Elk of the Ice Age

ALTICAMELUS 18 feet tall
A Giant Camel

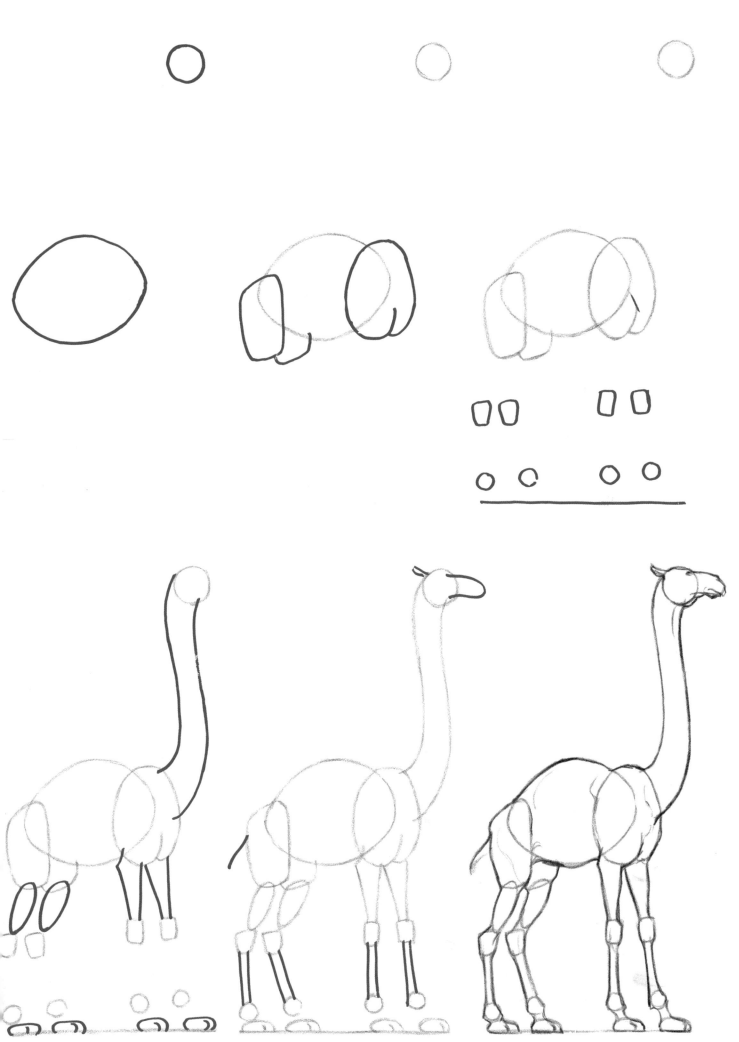

BALUCHITHERIUM   25 feet long
An Ancient Hornless Rhinoceros

WOOLLY MAMMOTH   10 feet tall
An Ice Age Elephant

ZEUGLODON   65 feet long

A Primitive Whale

BRONTOTHERIUM   15 feet long
An Early Hoofed Mammal, Related to Horses and Rhinoceroses

MEGATHERIUM   25 feet long
A Giant Ground Sloth

HYRACOTHERIUM (formerly EOHIPPUS)   1½ feet long
The Ancestor of the Horse

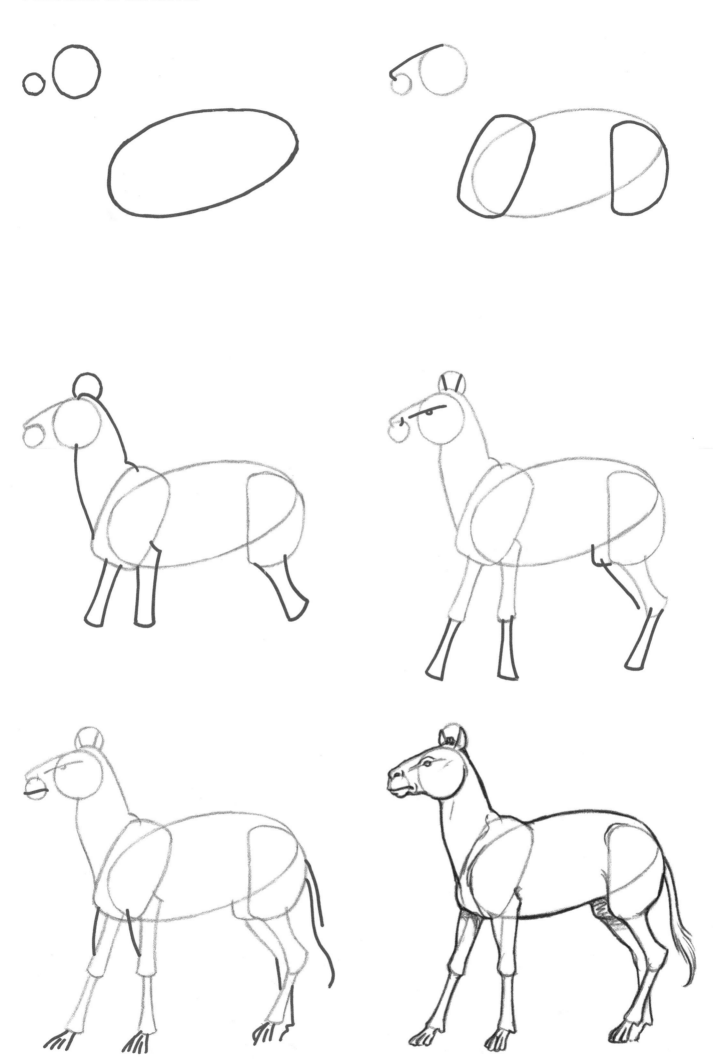

COELODONTA   12 feet long
The Woolly Rhinoceros of the Ice Ages

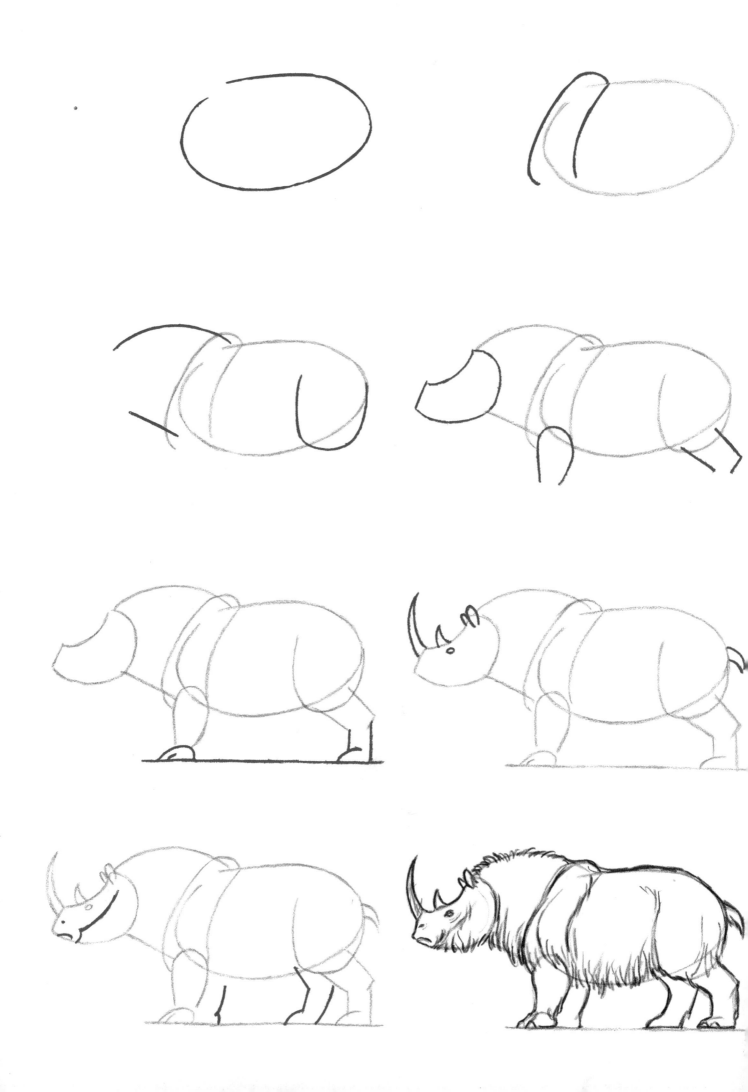